# Hollerin from This Shack

## Grace C. Ocasio

*aha*dada

**b o o k s**

tokyo / toronto

General Editor: Jesse Glass
Layout and design: Joe Zanghi, Printed Matter Press


editorial address:

3158 Bentworth Drive
Burlington, Ontario
Canada L7M-1M2


First Edition
Printed and Bound in Canada


ISBN 978-0-9812744-1-6

# Acknowledgements

The poem, "Little Brown Girl," appeared online courtesy of Bread and Lightning Press; the poem, "I Found Out," appeared in the literary journal *Court Green*; the poem, "Post-Reconstruction Blues," appeared in the anthology, *Step Up to the Mic: A Poetic Explosion*; the poetry journal *Main Street Rag* accepted "The Truth about Sherman"; the publication *The Poet Speaks* accepted "For Mother Hale"; the publication *Independence Boulevard* published the poem "To the Killers of the Dreamer, Dr. King: Dead or Alive"; the poetry publication *Iodine* accepted "For the Love of Men"; and the literary journal *Aries* published "Father Karamazov Speaks," now re-titled "Imagining Father Karamazov Speaking."

I'd like to thank my publisher Jesse Glass for his encouragement and patience during the revision phase of this chapbook project. I offer a special thanks to Diane Frank, chief editor of Blue Light Press, for her insightful critiques of several of the poems included in this chapbook. Very special thanks I extend to Lenard D. Moore and L. Teresa Church of the Carolina African American Writers' Collective for their ongoing support of my writing endeavors. I would also like to acknowledge my husband, Edwin, for urging me to pursue the writing life. Finally, I dedicate this chapbook to the memory of my mother, Ruby Louise Grant Waters, and my great-aunt, Ruby Funchess Johnston.

# Table of Contents

# Hollerin from This Shack

## I FOUND OUT

That the dimness of my circuits
Makes my whole face go blind.
I am prejudiced
Against myself.
I have a heart
Teeming with tar.

# THE HOLE

I have gone into this hole many times.
There's not much here
except a matchbook and a burnt out light bulb.

I do not think to throw out the light bulb,
souvenir that it is.
It reminds me of days
I sat in a room that swelled with light,
a room filled with dictionaries and encyclopedias.

I do not step into this room anymore
only because I burned it down
when I got tired of its brightness,

too bright with knowledge
that I could not absorb.

And in that room
dwell blackened words
trapped within charred notebooks.

Yet tonight I steal into that room,
park Indian style, blind as a TV screen
stacked with snow.

From this shack,
I seize matches, set 'em off,
to refute the light bulb, refute night.

## LITTLE BROWN GIRL

The child I gawked at in the picture is me.
I was five when I saw her face
in a '69 world yearbook.

With brown eyes and stringy black hair, arm
in a sling, she
had on a dress like a curtain. If I could hear her voice it would be
like a needle scratching a record.

She stared at me from the picture, pointed and asked,
"What are you doing in the south Bronx, in a
warm, cosy apartment?"

She made my engine snap.
I put the yearbook away
but whenever her face appears I spring out of sleep,
slide myself into the corner, face the window,
and cry out to the sky.

I mean I holler at that sky.

## TO AN OLD FRIEND

Little girl, I want
to stash you in my arms and blow away
all the bombs, bullets, and airplanes.

Especially those airplanes
that slit the sky's throat
then tried to rip you up,
into something like slices of bacon.

With my midget hands, I alone
will choke the planes.

They will land softly in trees
where they cannot hurt you.

# THE TRUTH ABOUT SHERMAN

I saw self-destruction's face
bound in reddish-brown colored skin.
We started dating in front of the mirror
where his eyes grumbled their tune of scotch and gin.

I'd ask him, "Are you ugly?"
He'd say yes. I'd say no.

So one day when
I could not seal him off from some claw of a man
who stole his money
then raked the blood out of his flesh, I cried.

Sherman,
the radiator in my room whispers your name,
and my fingers twirl your face round and round.

Tell me you're not like the snag in my rug.
Wave to me from the trees
or the ocean.

I will not find you in my bedroom
nor at my dinner table.

You are nothing
now
but the speck that eclipses my heart.

# ANYTHING BUT THIS

You said: "You only hear what you want to hear."

Not true, I hear letters. I hear nods.
I hear shudders.

And I heard your hands say three hundred dollars for an
    engagement ring is not enough.

I 'm tired of this,
Tired of talks that always lead to one of us being extinguished.

I'd rather be in a cell
Where I'd talk to the bars and floor and ceiling,
Anything but this.

The fact that your friend met the mayor of Mount Vernon is boring.
I just as well take notice of the maintenance man washing the
    co-op windows.

White Plains is boring. I want to go to Spain,
Meet a few chaps who can rap to me in Spanish,
See a few bullfights, shout olé,
Say good-bye to the amigos who have treated me to their country
    so well.

You, Mom, get stuck on the carpet.
Your feet are stubborn.
They station themselves in front of the magazine rack for hours.

I hate when you shuffle out of the dining room into the living
    room.
I wish you'd wear another pair of pants besides the ones that
    look like two sacks sewn together.

Even so, I see your dimple can still signal like a car light
When you go to your Bennett alumnae group.
But then you turn it off and won't turn it on again for weeks.

I'm tired of your slouches. So tired I've decided not to slouch.

I will walk and walk and walk.
In my dreams, I'm Grace Kelly walking up to the podium for
    an Oscar.

# ENGAGEMENT RING

The hands that never moved.
The dance never created.
A train on its way.
But like a derailed train,
It never arrived.

The gold ring in my dream
Floats in tub water.
Its diamond light
Flounces on tiled walls.

So now I sit here
On my beige rug
'Til my thighs itch
And my thumbs cramp.

Seize the phone, thump buttons
'Til my ears trace his tone.
"Give me the gift," I rasp.
Then I baptize his ears with a click.

Hours later, I hear the slosh of tires.
The rush of breath.
The squish of feet against steps.
Through the peephole, I spy
The glare of his flesh.

# THE DARK AGES

When I notice the wooden bowl
On my dining room table,
I wonder if I should use it as a weapon.
Should I pound the top of my head with it?
Or use it to knock somebody's teeth out with?

I do not remember
Or understand
That the bowl is for eating things in,
Like Cheerios or grits.

I'm tempted to throw my foot into it,
Thrashing my foot about,
Like a baby seal
Stuck within a tank of crude oil.

When I push my face against the bowl,
I gnaw on my name,
Chewing on each of its letters,
Like twigs.

And because I don't know
What to do with my name,
I deliver it to the ground.

In the Dark Ages,
I don't even know how to use a toilet.
So I shove my head into its porcelain vent,
Thinking the water will impede
My brain's retreat.

# WHAT THE SUN SAID

I was born when outer space was full
Of objects that glowed like cotton candy-
Bulbs shimmering in blue and orange hues,
Antennae tinged red, gold, white, and blue.

I saw gigantic fuchsia-colored webs.
The space was heavy then.
And now, space can no longer hold me.
Webs slit, cracked bulbs,
Faded antennae surround me.

I have wished I could go back in time,
When I was only an embryo of gas,
When the only thing
That lived beside me was the dark.

How tall the night was.
How the dark surrounded me, a fence-like womb.
The smell of night like grass.

And nothing could touch me.
The dark fed me.
Until I became a fully grown
Monolith of light,
The sun.

But then the ground split open and the people climbed out-
Hundreds, thousands.
Finally millions.

The rivers became unsettled
And strained towards the seas,
While the soil did nothing but slouch.
Now I slide around in space.
And whenever I see a man
I swerve
Out of his way.

# HIDDEN

The sun chooses to remain hidden,
jittery over the mothers
who wallop their sons in front of zookeepers,
panhandlers using their bodies as roadblocks
against subway riders.

The sun must be trying to tell me something.
"Don't come out today, Grace.
You may walk down the street
when someone decides to throw a brick at you,
no reason, just that you're walking pigeon-toed,
or wearing a blue blouse
with gray slacks
two colors that may annoy the person."

But I don't listen.
Instead I go out,
thinking my attacker may be on vacation today,
having decided to assault me when the sun comes out.

## SLIDING STAR

Do you hear the sun scratching the sky?
Smell the sun, like burning metal?
The sun like a police siren.
Listen to the sun's heart stutter,

Squint as the sun comes down like a plane,
Crashing on the ground
And hear the sun's metal clang,
Watch and bang your head on the pavement.
And you will splinter, like the sun.

# IMAGINING FATHER KARAMAZOV SPEAKING

Imagine you can summon
Into your living room
Dostoevsky's Fyodor Pavlovitch
And ask him why
He raped that idiot girl;
Of all the women
He could have chosen
To seduce
What did he see in her?
He'll probably say
Something like this:

"I needed something to do.
She was wandering around
In my courtyard.
And besides,
She reminded me
Of one of those mules some peasants own
With her eyes that can never quite
Place themselves
On another human being."

But when you ask him to describe
The feeling of knowing her,
He'll mutter,

"Being inside her is like slushing around
In the snow,
Nothing like
Being with a beautiful woman
Who makes you feel like
You're stepping onto a Persian rug
In your bare feet."

Imagine, then, that you are alone in your study,
Your mind spreading wide open
The page of the victim.
Sunlight drifts across her page.

## FOR THE LOVE OF MEN

If I could I would repair
All the hearts of men
That have been crippled for years
By women who have stomped on them.

Here's to the men who danced
Naked in the desert
And were glad they could bare
Their chests to the sun
And know what made them humble
And what lies strangled between their legs.

Here's for the men who carry their souls
In their hands
And weep for them.
To the men young and old
I kiss you.
And I tuck inside me your seed.

# IMAGINE

the breath of all the midgets and puppets.
Move to the breath of a boy
who got knocked down by an ironing board
when only two years old.

The breath of sickness,
a number repeating itself.
Poverty's breath,
the man unable to soothe his fingers
to sleep.

# FOR MOTHER HALE

She was four years old
When she told her mother
She wanted a baby bad.

Her wish came up to her
When she wrung out two babies of her own.
Then her wish approached her again

When forty other children
Stationed themselves on her front doorsteps
Seven days a week for years.

Someone who doesn't know her
Might wonder why
After all those kids

Did she decide to take on
A bunch of drug-addicted ones.
Someone might wonder

What was she doing with them.
She was just
Handing out the glance of her smile

So that each one of her hundreds absorbed it.
Like Cracker Jacks
She shook them up and down

Shaking some music
A little Coltrane
And a bit of the Duke

Into them.
She was just taking her fingers
And massaging the crack out of their veins.

She said
She wasn't gonna die not doing.
And she didn't.

## TO THE KILLERS OF THE DREAMER, DR. KING: DEAD OR ALIVE

I could tell you why
I'd like my breath to ram
Through the window in my room like a bullet.
But would you listen?

Listen to the sound of my voice
Like a blender mashing up tomatoes.

My voice
Swallowing up your eardrums.
Then the breath in your lungs and your mouth.

Would let you go.
Dried out.
Like an overcooked steak.

I would carry you out in a crate.
Offer you to the stars or the moon.

# POST-RECONSTRUCTION BLUES

One day I noticed oppression
Squatting in the corner of my room.

I was six years old when I first realized
I was only two inches above it.

That's when grandma told me
About the sharecropper
Who was my grandfather
Who had to unstoop his shoulders
Just to look up at
His papier mâché-skinned boss
Who held scrip money in his hand.

Grandpa's bones crackled
To snap themselves into place
So he stood
Erect as a cat's tail.

Grandma's voice climbed through me
When she said:
"And just before
Your granddaddy's fingers
Reached up for the scrip
It was then, child,
That his neck discovered
The electricity stashed
Inside a noose."

Grandma's words still cling to me like oil.

# MEN IN THE STREET

Men. Men. All over.
Hiding in potholes. Hiding in gutters.
Try to grab my ankles as I walk down the street.
I kick their noses.
Remember. They're underground.

Sometimes they're in the sky,
In the shape of a face with two bowlike eyebrows
And a boomerang grin.
I never let them rummage through me with their eyes.

Eyes like candlesticks. Too long. Too narrow.
I want to deflate them.
Press a button and puff go their eyes.

Want to see them all turn into midgets,
Bounce their heads like a basketball,
Spin them round and round
And put them up through the rim.
Swish.

Then their grins would slouch on their faces,
Fall off and float into the ocean,
Swirl down to its bottom,
Where they'd be doomed to drink sea dregs.

# ELEGY FOR SHOPPING CARTS

Each time I go to the grocery store
I ask my fingers what can they do
For the shopping carts turned on their sides
In the corners of the parking lot
Or left to sail into the street.

All too easily I befriend them
When shoppers leave them loose
In the way of motorists
Who slam on their brakes too late.

And then pieces of their bodies end up
Scattered across the baffled road.

If only all these soulless shoppers
Would treat the carts as they would
A pair of velvet gloves or a silk tie
Instead of the clunky pieces of metal that they are.

## LIFE IN THE SUBURBS

I've often asked myself if I really exist
Knowing my life comes within
Seconds of being snatched from me by drivers
Who ram their cars into my car's space.

I've got a hunch—either their brains have been confiscated
By the IRS
Or been stored in some wine cellar in Italy.

I never detect a trickle of repentance
Spilling from the muscles of their faces—
Nothing more than rags before my eyes.
I don't bother to ask the sky
Whether or not it has permission to stay up there,
Realizing it could come down on my head
Like an elevator,
Sending me reeling me into the next life.

I've never tested if the arms
Or legs of people I pass
On my way to Macy's are alive
By aiming my handbag at their heads.
I never step over milk crates,
Thinking them hazardous to my health.
I pray the ground will remain impartial to my weight.

I'd like to trade my hands in—
Maybe for ferrets,
Ferrets fastened to my wrists.

Each ferret of each arm would do nothing
But scowl when greeting people in malls.
I can only wonder how
And if their hands would react.

## ON LADY DAY

Billie Holiday's voice
inscribes its tears onto each cell of my body.

My body is too hollow to respond.
And my soul too thin to prop her voice up like a lift.

My skin's never stung from the whip of a lover's hand,
never heard the lurch of whiskey from a lover's lips,
I, who lived like a half slip
nine years in a royal blue house on a hill,
sequestered from my neighbors.

I put her voice back into its crawl space
where it slouches,
like an emaciated slug.
I tuck it in.
Warm it with my breasts.

Breathe on it.
Let it inhale the years that have fallen
like a broom on a child's leg.

If you take her voice out,
you will see tears the size of grapefruits
whirling down from the sky.

## About the Author

Grace Ocasio is a member of the North Carolina Writers' Network, the North Carolina Poetry Society, and the Carolina African American Writers' Collective. She lives in Charlotte, North Carolina, with her husband, Edwin. She was born in New York City and raised in Hartsdale and White Plains, New York. She holds an MFA in Poetry from Sarah Lawrence College and an MA in English from the University of North Carolina at Charlotte. Recently, she completed a residency at the Soul Mountain Retreat in East Haddam, Connecticut. Besides writing poetry, she contributes reviews of literary journals to the online Web site, *The Review, Review.*

# OTHER TITLES FROM AHADADA

*Ahadada Books publishes poetry. Preserving the best of the small press tradition, we produce finely designed and crafted books in limited editions.*

## Bela Fawr's Cabaret (David Annwn)                978-0-9808873-2-7

Writes Gavin Selerie: "David Annwn's work drills deep into strata of myth and history,. exposing devices which resonate in new contexts. Faithful to the living moment, his poems dip, hover and dart through soundscapes rich with suggestion, rhythmically charged and etymologically playful. Formally adventurous and inviting disjunction, these texts retain a lyric coherence that powerfully renders layers of experience. The mode veers from jazzy to mystical, evoking in the reader both disturbance and content. *Bela Fawr's Cabaret* has this recognisable stamp: music and legend 'Knocked Abaht a Bit', mischievous humour yielding subtle insight."

## Age of the Demon Tools (Mark Spitzer)                978-0-9808873-1-0

Writes Ed Sanders: "You have to slow down, and absorb calmly, the procession of gritty, pointillist gnarls of poesy that Mark Spitzer wittily weaves into his book. Just the title, *Age of the Demon Tools*, is so appropriate in this horrid age of inappropriate technology—you know, corruptly programmed voting machines, drones with missiles hovering above huts, and mind reading machines looming just a few years into the demon-tool future. When you do slow down, and tarry within Spitzer's neologism-packed litanies, you will find the footprints of bards such as Allen Ginsberg, whose tradition of embedding current events into the flow of poesy is one of the great beacons of the new century. This book is worth reading if only for the poem 'Unholy Millenial Litany' and its blastsome truths."

## Sweet Potatoes (Lou Rowan)                978-0-9781414-5-5

Lou Rowan . . . is retired, in love and charged. He was raised by horse breeders and went to Harvard and thus possesses an outward polish. But he talks like a radical, his speech incongruous with his buttoned-down appearance. *Golden Handcuffs Review*, the local literary magazine that Rowan founded and edits, is much like the man himself: appealing and presentable on the outside, a bit wild and experimental at the core.

## Deciduous Poems (David B. Axelrod)                978-0-9808873-0-3

Dr. David B. Axelrod has published hundreds of articles and poems as well as sixteen books of poetry. Among his many grants and awards, he is recipient of three Fulbright Awards including his being the first official Fulbright Poet-in-Residence in the People's Republic of China. He was featured in Newsday as a "Star in his academic galaxy," and characterized by the New York Times as "a treat." He has shared the stage with such notables as Louis Simpson, X. J. Kennedy, William Stafford, Robert Bly, Allen Ginsburg, David Ignatow and Galway Kinnell, in performance for the U.N., the American Library Association, the Struga Festival, and hundreds more schools and public events. His poetry has been translated into fourteen languages and he is a frequent and celebrated master teacher.

## Late Poems of Lu You (Burton Watson)                978-0-9781414-9-3

Lu You (1125–1210) whose pen name was 'The Old Man Who Does as He Pleases,' was among the most prolific of Chinese poets, having left behind a collection of close to ten thousand poems as well as miscellaneous prose writings. His poetry, often characterized by an intense patriotism, is also notable for its recurrent expression of a carefree enjoyment of life. This volume consists of twenty-five of Burton Watson's new translations, plus Lu You's poems as they appear in the original, making this a perfect collection for the lay reader as well as for those with a mastery of Song dynasty Chinese.

**www.ahadadabooks.com**

## Oulipoems (Philip Terry)                 978-0-978-1414-2-4

Philip Terry was born in Belfast in 1962 and has been working with Oulipian and related writing practices for over twenty years. His lipogrammatic novel *The Book of Bachelors* (1999), was highly praised by the Oulipo: "Enormous rigour, great virtuosity—but that's the least of it." Currently he is Director of Creative Writing at the University of Essex, where he teaches a graduate course on the poetics of constraint. His work has been published in *Panurge*, *PN Review*, *Oasis*, *North American Review* and *Onedit*, and his books include the celebrated anthology of short stories *Ovid Metamorphosed* (2000) and *Fables of Aesop* (2006). His translation of Raymond Queneau's last book of poems, *Elementary Morality*, is forthcoming from Carcanet. *Oulipoems* is his first book of poetry.

## The Impossibility of Dreams (David Axelrod)                 978-0-9781414-3-1

Writes Louis Simpson: "Whether Axelrod is reliving a moment of pleasure, or a time of bitterness and pain, the truth of his poetry is like life itself compelling." Dr. David B. Axelrod has published hundreds of articles and poems as well as sixteen books of poetry. Among his many grants and awards, he is recipient of three Fulbright Awards including his being the first official Fulbright Poet-in-Residence in the People's Republic of China . He was featured in *Newsday* as a "Star in his academic galaxy," and characterized by the *New York Times* as "A Treat." His poetry has been translated into fourteen languages and he is a frequent and celebrated master teacher.

## Now Showing (Jim Daniels)                 0-9781414-1-5

Of Jim Daniels, the *Harvard Review* writes, "Although Daniels' verse is thematically dark, the energy and beauty of his language and his often brilliant use of irony affirm that a lighter side exists. This poet has already found his voice. And he speaks with that rare urgency that demands we listen." This is affirmed by Carol Muske, who identifies the "melancholy sweetness" running through these poems that identifies him as "a poet born to praise".

## China Notes & The Treasures of Dunhuang (Jerome Rothenberg)   0-9732233-9-1

"*The China Notes* come from a trip in 2002 that brought us out as far as the Gobi Desert & allowed me to see some of the changes & continuities throughout the country. I was traveling with poet & scholar Wai-lim Yip & had a chance to read poetry in five or six cities & to observe things as part of an ongoing discourse with Wai-lim & others. The ancient beauty of some of what we saw played out against the theme park quality of other simulacra of the past....A sense of beckoning wilderness/wildness in a landscape already cut into to serve the human need for power & control." So Jerome Rothenberg describes the events behind the poems in this small volume—a continuation of his lifelong exploration of poetry and the search for a language to invoke the newness and strangeness both of what we observe and what we can imagine.

## The Passion of Phineas Gage & Selected Poems (Jesse Glass)                 0-9732233-8-3

*The Passion of Phineas Gage & Selected Poems* presents the best of Glass' experimental writing in a single volume. Glass' ground-breaking work has been hailed by poets as diverse as Jerome Rothenberg, William Bronk and Jim Daniels for its insight into human nature and its exploration of forms. Glass uses the tools of postmodernism: collaging, fragmentation, and Oulipo-like processes along with a keen understanding of poetic forms and traditions that stretches back to Beowulf and beyond. Moreover, Glass finds his subject matter in larger-than-life figures like Phineas Gage—the man whose life was changed in an instant when an iron bar was sent rocketing through his brain in a freak accident—as well as in ants processing up a wall in time to harpsichord music in order to steal salt crystals from the inner lip of a cowrie shell. The range and ambition of his work sets it apart. The product of over 30 years of engagement with the avant-garde, *The Passion of Phineas Gage & Selected Poems* is the work of a mature poet who continues to reinvent himself with every text he produces.

# www.ahadadabooks.com

Send a request to be added to our mailing list:
http://www.ahadadabooks.com

**Ahadada Books are available from these fine distributors:**

**Canada**
Ahadada Books
3158 Bentworth Drive
Burlington, Ontario
Canada, L7M 1M2
Tel: (905) 617-7754
http://www.ahadadabooks.com/

**United States of America**
Small Press Distribution
1341 Seventh Street
Berkeley, CA
U.S.A. 94710-1409
Tel: (510) 524-1668
Fax: (510) 524-0852
http://www.spdbooks.org/

**Europe**
West House Books
40 Crescent Road
Nether Edge, Sheffield
United Kingdom  S7 1HN
Tel: 0114-2586035
http://www.westhousebooks.co.uk/

**Japan**
Printed Matter Press
Yagi Bldg. 4F, 2-10-13 Shitaya,
Taito-ku, Tokyo
Japan 110-0004
Tel: 81-3-3876-8766
Fax: 81-3-3871-4964
http://www.printedmatterpress.com/